SAMUEL BARBER

SONATA
for
PIANO

ISBN 978-0-634-02624-9

Ed. 1971

G. SCHIRMER, Inc.

DISTRIBUTED BY
HAL•LEONARD®
CORPORATION
7777 W. BLUEMOUND RD. P.O. BOX 13819 MILWAUKEE, WI 53213

Commissioned by The League of Composers

for its twenty-fifth anniversary

Sonata for Piano

Samuel Barber, Op. 26

12

Tempo I°

18

II

Allegro vivace e leggero ♩. = 152

III

IV

Fuga

giocoso, ma sempre a tempo